Welcome!

Families use many ways to remember their best stories. Maybe your family has photo albums and old diaries or letters. Maybe you have a trunk full of family keepsakes in the attic, a lace tablecloth your great-grandmother made, or a sausage recipe your grandfather passed on.

You have probably heard the same family stories told again and again at Christmas or on birthdays and anniversaries. The stories stay alive in the telling. They are remembered and handed down by each new generation.

You may be a story keeper already. Perhaps you are collecting stories of your own life. Perhaps you save your baby book in your room, or help your mom frame your school pictures and hang them in the hallway, or protect a scrapbook or a diary under lock and key, or store a ratty teddy bear or worn-out Cabbage Patch doll on the top shelf of the closet, or own a sealed box of stuff you haven't looked at for over a year. This could be *your* way of keeping your story—of remembering.

When Jesus was about your age, he knew the stories of his Jewish family. The traditions and tales he inherited were told and then written in scrolls called the Jewish Scriptures. Today we call these scriptures the Old Testament.

In this course you learn how the Old Testament is put together and you study some of the great stories Jesus knew. You explore the following people and events:

- Adam and Eve, God's Creation, and the response of the first human beings to God's invitation to friendship

- Abraham and Sarah and their family—the first family of faith

- Moses, who led the Israelites to freedom

- David, the great king of Israel

- the Old Testament prophets, who called the people of God to faith-filled action

As you study the great and ancient stories of the Jewish people, you can also discover the deep roots of the story of Jesus and of those who claim to follow him, Christians. And in doing that you can discover your own story as well.

For Sure!

How can we know who God is? How can we know what God really and truly cares about?

If we look at a newborn baby or a sunset or a mountain, we might guess about the Creator of all this wonder. Many people in ancient times did just this. They thought that many gods created many wonders. They believed in a god of water, a god who ruled the seas, a god who governed the skies, and on and on.

It seems that the only way we can know who God is for sure, is to learn about God from God. That is, we can learn the truth about God only through God's self-revelation. The word *revelation* means "a showing" or "a telling." The Bible shows and tells us this: God seeks a relationship with us, and God is on our side. We can be sure of these two huge truths because God has revealed them to us.

The Bible is made up of two sets of writings that are all inspired by God and all tell about God. These two main sections of the Bible are the Old Testament and the New Testament. The books of the Old Testament

contain many kinds of writings: family stories, national histories, prayers, warnings, dreams and visions, and wise sayings. These writings reveal the truth about God and the people of Israel before Jesus was born. They help us understand who God is, and also that we are invited to live as a people God calls and cares for. The New Testament continues the story of Israel as it unfolds after the birth of Jesus.

Key Understandings

Basic Facts About the Bible

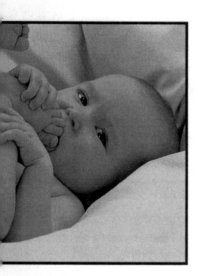

- The Bible is divided into two main sections: the Old Testament and the New Testament.
- The Old Testament makes up the largest part of the Bible, and the New Testament makes up the smallest.
- The Old Testament tells the story of God's relationship with the Jewish people up to the time of Jesus.
- The Old Testament also helps us understand the New Testament.
- The New Testament tells the story of Jesus and his followers.

Bible Facts

- The Old Testament was written over the course of about a thousand years; the New Testament was written over the course of about a hundred years.
- For hundreds of years, the people of Israel passed on their family stories by word of mouth. This is called their oral, or spoken, tradition.
- The word *scripture* means "writings." Sometimes the Bible is called holy Scriptures or holy writings.
- There were at least four major authors of the Old Testament. God's inspiration guided their writing.
- The first words of the Old Testament were written on parchment made of goatskin or sheepskin. The parchment was rolled into scrolls. Many of the scrolls were stored in clay jars. These jars kept out the moisture and strong sunlight that would have faded and spoiled the parchment.

THE STORY OF ISRAEL

OLD TESTAMENT

Genesis
Exodus
Leviticus
Numbers
Deuteronomy
Joshua
Judges
Ruth
1 Samuel
2 Samuel
1 Kings
2 Kings
1 Chronicles
2 Chronicles
Ezra
Nehemiah
Tobit
Judith
Esther
1 Maccabees
2 Maccabees

WISDOM BOOKS

Job
Psalms
Proverbs
Ecclesiastes
Song of Songs
Wisdom
Sirach
   (or Ecclesiasticus)

PROPHETIC BOOKS

Isaiah
Jeremiah
Lamentations
Baruch
Ezekiel
Daniel
Hosea
Joel
Amos
Obadiah
Jonah
Micah
Nahum
Habakkuk
Zephaniah
Haggai
Zechariah
Malachi

NEW TESTAMENT

GOSPELS

Matthew
Mark
Luke
John

Acts of the Apostles
Romans
1 Corinthians
2 Corinthians
Galatians
Ephesians
Philippians
Colossians
1 Thessalonians
2 Thessalonians
1 Timothy
2 Timothy
Titus
Philemon
Hebrews
James
1 Peter
2 Peter
1 John
2 John
3 John
Jude
Revelation

Original Blessing

THE PEOPLE OF ISRAEL TOLD A STORY ABOUT THEIR GOD AS LORD OF all the universe. They believed that the God of Israel created everything and found it all very good.

The people believed that in the best possible world, each and every creature came forth from God's hand and received God's blessing. Each was commanded to grow and spread and fill the earth.

This Creation story was Israel's very own family faith story. The people could easily remember this story, for it followed a seven-day pattern.

God's Creation began on the first day, in darkness and confusion. God called light into being, and there was light. Then each day dawned more beautiful than the one before it and was filled with amazing creatures.

On the sixth day, human beings were made in God's image and likeness. They were God's finishing touch. God gave them the task of caring for the earth and keeping it new and fresh.

And then God stopped. The seventh day was set aside to be a day of joy and peace. It was a holy day, a day for all Creation to rest and be with God.

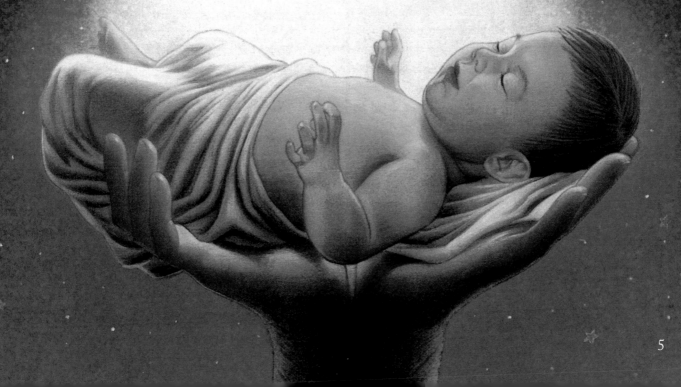

A New Song

This song is from the Book of Psalms of the Old Testament. It tells of creation, and praises the wonderful order of God's creation and our place in it.

Key Understandings
The First Creation Story

- The God of Israel is the Creator of the world.
- God finds all of creation good.
- Human beings are made in God's image and likeness.
- Human beings are responsible for caring for the world.
- Human beings are given one day in seven to rest in God.

¹ O God, our God,
How glorious is your name over all the earth!
Your glory is praised in the heavens.

² Out of the mouths of children and babes
you have fashioned praise . . .
. . . .

³ When I look at your heavens, the work of your hands,
the moon and the stars which you created—

⁴ who are we that you should be mindful of us,
that you should care for us?

⁵ You have made us a little less than the gods
and crowned us with glory and honor.

⁶ You have given us rule over the works of your hands,
putting all things under our feet:

⁷ all sheep and oxen,
yes, and the beasts of the field;

⁸ the birds of the air, the fishes of the sea,
and whatever swims the paths of the seas.

⁹ God, our God,
how glorious is your name over all the earth!

(Psalm 8, from Nancy Schreck and Maureen Leach, Psalms Anew, page 23)

Our Place

The Hebrew people developed a second Creation story, which helped them explain how sin and loss came into the world. This story can be found in Genesis, chapters 2 to 3. In it God created human beings a little lower than the gods. God then created a perfect garden of delights. But a tempter moved through the garden, in the form of a serpent. And the serpent challenged the first human beings, Adam and Eve, to think about their place in God's created world. Adam and Eve had to choose between the tempter and God.

Adam and Eve chose the tempter and lost their friendship with God, their Creator. They also lost their harmony with the created world. The Old Testament records a long human struggle with sin and loss and our need for a redeemer. Christians believe that Jesus is the obedient Son of God who cancels the disobedience of Adam. Jesus is the redeemer who overcomes sin and brings us back to the full life with God that was lost in the Garden of Eden.

Paradise

In the beginning a stream of water flowed across the empty land. There God knelt down and formed Adam from the clay of the ground.

Then God planted a garden called Eden. It was beautiful to see. It was filled with all good foods to eat. A single tree of wisdom grew in the center of the garden. This tree gave knowledge of what was good and what was evil, and it was for God alone. Everything else was for Adam's delight.

God wanted more for Adam. So God created birds to fill the air and fishes to fill the sea and animals to roam the earth. Adam named all the animals.

Even with all that God had given him, Adam was still lonely. So God created Eve to be his partner and life companion.

Temptation

One day a clever serpent drew near to Eve. The serpent convinced Eve to try the fruit from the one tree that was God's alone. Eve saw how good this fruit would be to eat, and thought how wonderful it would be to be wise. The serpent said: "You do not have to obey God. Why, you can even replace God! Think of that! You can know evil and good, just as God does."

Loss

So Eve ate some of the fruit, and she gave some to Adam. At that moment they knew they had disobeyed God. They were so ashamed they hid in the deepest part of the garden, far, far away from God.

At sundown, when the evening breezes stirred, God called out to Adam and asked him why he was hiding. Adam answered that Eve had made him eat the fruit of the tree of wisdom. Then God asked Eve why she had done that. Eve replied that the serpent had tricked her into eating the fruit.

Adam and Eve had turned the beauty and the order of Creation upside down. They did not want to be "a little less than the gods." They tried to be smarter and greater than God, rather than grateful children of God. Their choice meant that they lost the joy of God's familiar presence.

The garden was no longer a place of ease and rest. Adam and Eve and all human beings after them would have to work hard to harvest the goods of the earth. They would experience pain as they bore and raised their children. They would have to struggle to overcome pride and selfishness. They had lost the Paradise God had given them.

Key Understandings

The Second Creation Story

- God gives us the freedom to choose.
- We find our happiness in faithful obedience to God.
- Sin is the human failure to be obedient servants of God.

STANDING *Tall*

1. In this space draw or describe your own paradise, the place or time in which you are happy with yourself and at peace with God.

2. Here is a collection of things that especially appeal to young people. On the blank lines, add other things that tempt you.

NEAT CLOTHES

FRIENDS

POPULARITY

GOOD GRADES

POWER

INDEPENDENCE

EXTRA MONEY

<u>FAMILY</u>

ATHLETIC ABILITY

<u>PHONE</u>   <u>Normal</u>

3. What are people your age willing to do, or not do, to get the things that tempt them?

Work hard, bug parents, annoy family, pay for it, do chores, babysit, do jobs, car wash

4. Think of a time when you stood up and did the right thing. On the card your teacher has given you, write about how you stood tall, and kept your friendship with God and your pride about yourself.

Bible Facts

- Although the two Creation stories appear in the very beginning of the Bible, they were not written down until very late in Jewish history.
- The Jewish people lived among other tribes, who believed in many gods—gods of the water, the forest, the sky, and so on. The Jewish people believed in one God who is Lord of all. The first Creation story expresses this deep belief.
- God created Adam, or "man," from clay, or soil. The name Adam is based on the Hebrew word for soil, which is *damah*. In the second Creation story, the words *Adam* and *damah* are closely related. They remind us that we are of the earth.
- The Apostle Paul spoke of Adam as the one whose actions brought sin to the world. Paul portrayed Jesus as a new Adam who brought redemption and salvation to the world. "For just as in Adam all die, so too in Christ shall all be brought to life" (1 Corinthians 15:22).

GOD'S FIRST FAMILY

The Jewish people told many stories about the first people on the earth. By and by these stories were written down and became the Book of Genesis. In this book we read how Cain was jealous of his brother, Abel, and killed him. We learn how God ordered Noah to build an ark and to save the creatures on earth. We learn how the earth was re-created after the Great Flood.

One well-loved story of two great heroes of faith that was told for hundreds of years before it was written down in the Book of Genesis is the story of Abraham and Sarah.

Long ago and far away, in the land of Ur, near the mouth of the Tigris and Euphrates Rivers, there lived Abram and his wife Sarai. God called Abram and said:

"Go forth from the land of your kinsfolk and from your father's house to a land that I will show you."

(Genesis 12:1)

Read Genesis 12:2 and write down God's Promise to Abram.

_____

_____

_____

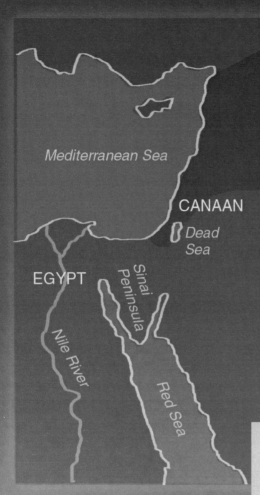

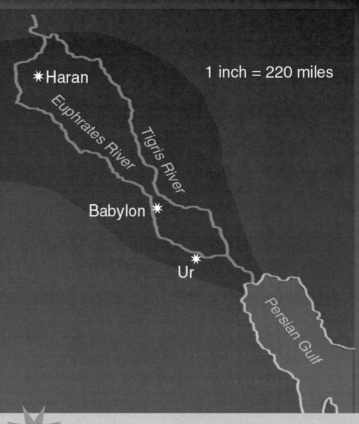

1 inch = 220 miles

Mediterranean Sea

Haran

Euphrates River

Tigris River

CANAAN

Dead Sea

Babylon

EGYPT

Sinai Peninsula

Ur

Nile River

Red Sea

Persian Gulf

Abram and his wife Sarai and their family obeyed God. They left their home in Ur. For years they journeyed on and on. They grew weary and discouraged. They wondered if they would ever reach the new land that God had promised them. Also, Abram and Sarai wanted a child, but they were getting old and their hope for one was dwindling.

All day long they saw the grains of sand underfoot; all night long they saw the stars twinkling overhead. They kept on going and believing and waiting and remembering God's Promise.

When Abram was almost one hundred years old, God addressed him again and gave him a new name.

✶ Read Genesis 17:5. What did God change Abram's name to?

_____

✶ Who or what did God promise to make him the father of?

_____

✶ Read Genesis 17:7. Who did God intend to make a covenant with?

_____

✶ How long did God say the relationship, or covenant, would last?

_____

✶ Read Genesis 17:15. What did God change Sarai's name to?

_____

✶ Read Genesis 22:17. God said that Abraham and Sarah's children would be as countless as what?

_____

At long last Sarah had a child. She and Abraham named him Isaac, which means "laugh." Thus, the family of Abraham and Sarah began with a Promise that was fulfilled through a joyful laugh. God's first family was glad. God remained faithful, and Abraham and Sarah remained faithful too. They believed that God was with and for them.

Abraham and Sarah's son Isaac grew up and married Rebekah. Isaac and Rebekah's son Jacob became the father of twelve sons. God gave Jacob the new name Israel. Jacob's sons became the twelve tribes of Israel. And thus God's Promise to Abraham and Sarah was fulfilled.

The First Family Tree

The family tree of Abraham and Sarah shows how God's Promise to them was finally fulfilled.

Zebulun

Issachar

Reuben

Simeon

Benjamin

Dan

Naphtali

Gad

Judah

Joseph

Asher

Levi

Leah

Rachel

Bilhah

Zilpah

Jacob

Isaac and Rebekah

Abraham and Sarah

Key Understandings

God's First Family
- Abraham and Sarah were heroes of faith.
- Abraham and Sarah believed and trusted in God's Promise.
- God's Promise to Abraham and Sarah was fulfilled through the birth of their son Isaac.
- The twelve sons of Isaac's son Jacob, or Israel, grew to become twelve large tribes, called the tribes of Israel.

An ENSLAVED PEOPLE

The twelve sons in the family of Jacob, or Israel, grew and prospered in Canaan. The oldest sons were jealous of the youngest son, Joseph. Jacob favored Joseph and gave Joseph a beautiful coat. The eleven older brothers never received such a rich gift.

Joseph dreamed that his brothers would one day bow before him. He told his brothers about the dream. This was just too much for his brothers to take. They wanted to get rid of Joseph, so they sold him to Egyptian traders who were traveling through the area. Then the brothers lied and told their father that Joseph had died.

Joseph grew up in the court of Pharaoh. From there he managed the storehouses and food supplies of the land of the Nile. And he did a good job; his skill was known far and wide. Everyone in the country was healthy and happy.

After many years a great famine struck the land. Because of Joseph's leadership, Egypt had food for its people, but in Canaan there was no food. The eleven older sons of Jacob grew so hungry that they eventually went to Egypt in search of grain. Joseph recognized his brothers when they appeared before him. He forgave them for what they had done to him, and welcomed them to Egypt.

As the years rolled by, the families of Jacob's sons grew to great numbers. The Egyptian people feared that the tribes of Jacob would soon outnumber them. So the Egyptians took away all the tribes' land and rights and made the children of Jacob work as slaves. The Egyptians called these people *apiru*, which means "the people from nowhere."

As time passed the Hebrews forgot they were God's people. They forgot they were sons and daughters of the once-proud twelve tribes of Israel. They felt they were just slaves from nowhere. It would be hundreds of years before their slavery would end.

(This story is based on Genesis 35; 37; 39—46:8.)

Journey to Freedom

1. Holy Ground

Read Exodus 3:1–5. God cared for the large, enslaved family of Abraham and Sarah. Moses learned that God remembered the people and the faith of the ancestors. As a group describe the place where Moses had his vision of God. Discuss how Moses showed his reverence for the holy place where God appeared.

Read Exodus 3:6–8 to find out who God is and what God planned to do for the Hebrew people.

Read Exodus 3:13–15 to find out what Moses was to tell the Hebrew people. As a group discuss what God planned to do for the people.

Use the lines below to describe a place that is holy for you. This can be a place where you go to seek comfort and peace. It can be your own holy ground, a special place where you can think and talk to God.

2. Trouble in Egypt

Pharaoh would not listen to Moses' plea, "Let my people go!" Instead of releasing the Hebrews, he made work harder and harder for them. He forced them to make more and more bricks out of less and less straw and mud.

Soon everything seemed to go wrong in Egypt. First, small disturbances occurred. Then things got worse and worse and troubles piled up. These troubles are called the Ten Plagues. You can read about them in Exodus, chapters 7 to 11.

The Egyptians thought these plagues were a sign that they should let the Hebrews go free. Finally, Pharaoh released Moses' people.

3. The Great Escape

When the Israelites reached the edge of the Red Sea, they became frightened and worried. They could hear the waves on the shore. They feared the armies of Egypt coming from behind. They were unsure about what to do.

We also have problems, fears, and troubles. We also worry and are unsure. We face our own version of the Red Sea. Think about the following sentence-starters. On the lines below them, write your response to at least one of them.

- The biggest trouble I have with my parents is . . .
- My friends and I seem to struggle hardest about . . .
- At school the battle I fight all the time is . . .
- The toughest battle I'm fighting right now is . . .

At school the battle I fight all the time is keeping my grades up.

17

4. A Covenanted People

The God of Abraham and Isaac and Jacob acted on the side of the Israelites. The Lord who appeared to Moses brought them to freedom through the Red Sea.

Then God made a Covenant on Mount Sinai. This Sinai Covenant called the people of Israel to be God's own people. It showed them how to be God's Covenant people. God told the people:

"I, the LORD, am your God, who brought you out of the land of Egypt, that place of slavery." (Exodus 20:2)

1. I am the LORD your God: you shall not have strange Gods before me.

2. You shall not take the name of the LORD your God in vain.

3. Remember to keep holy the LORD's Day.

4. Honor your father and your mother.

5. You shall not kill.

6. You shall not commit adultery.

7. You shall not steal.

8. You shall not bear false witness against your neighbor.

9. You shall not covet your neighbor's wife.

10. You shall not covet your neighbor's goods.

(Exodus 20:2–17, as adapted in *Catechism of the Catholic Church*, pages 496–497)

Bible Facts

- Religious leaders in Israel taught that the Ten Commandments were the decrees that established God's relationship with the Israelites. The leaders added so many rules to the Covenant, or Law of Moses, that people found them hard to understand and follow.
- Jesus said that he came to fulfill the Law of Moses. He also helped the people of God understand and be faithful to the Law of Moses. He said, "'Do to others whatever you would have them do to you'" (Matthew 7:12).
- Jesus was once asked which of the Commandments was the greatest. He answered: "'You shall love the Lord, your God, with all your heart, with all your soul, and with all your mind. . . . You shall love your neighbor as yourself. The whole law and the prophets depend on these two commandments'" (Matthew 22:37–40).
- Jesus spoke of the new and eternal covenant when he offered the bread and wine at the Last Supper. This New Covenant was the new relationship between God and humanity established through Jesus' life, death, and Resurrection.
- Catholics understand the event of Jesus' Passion, death, and Resurrection as the New Passover. His "passing over" from death to life is called the paschal mystery. In the celebration of the sacraments, Catholics share in this mystery. The paschal mystery is celebrated in a special way during Holy Week and during the Easter, or paschal, season.

Key Understandings

God's Call to a Covenant Relationship

- The God of Moses is revealed as the God of Abraham, Isaac, and Jacob.
- God promised to act on the side of the Hebrew people.
- Through Moses, God led the Israelites from slavery to freedom.
- God made a Covenant with the people of Israel.
- The Ten Commandments teach that God is our God.
- The Ten Commandments teach us how to be God's people.

Live in God's Love

The Covenant I have made with you is not a great mystery. It is not beyond your reach.

It is not flung out into the sky among the stars. You do not need to wonder who will go to heaven and bring it near.

The Covenant is not far beyond the seas. You do not need to search for someone to cross the water and bring it to you.

No, the Covenant is as near as the words of your mouth, as close as your heart.

I set before you life and death. Choose life, then, that you may live in the love of your God, hold fast to your Lord.

(Adapted from Deuteronomy 30:11–20)

A New King for Israel

God called the holy man Samuel to take scented oil and travel to Bethlehem to the house of Jesse. God told Samuel that his mission was to anoint one of Jesse's sons to be the next king of Israel.

Samuel set out as the Lord commanded.

Jesse welcomed Samuel and put on a great feast. His seven oldest sons gathered around the table. One by one Jesse presented his sons to Samuel.

Each time Jesse thought: "This must be the one. He is handsome and healthy."

But each time Samuel said, "No, he is not the one."

Finally, Samuel asked if there was another son. Jesse said, "Yes, my youngest son is out in the fields tending the sheep."

"Send for him this minute!" Samuel commanded.

When the youngest son arrived, Samuel knew he was the one. He was handsome and healthy. His eyes sparkled with life. Samuel immediately anointed the youngest son, and God's spirit rushed upon the boy. The young man's name was David.

(Adapted from 1 Samuel 16:1–3)

Consider

DAVID

SHEPHERD

SINNER

MUSICIAN

KING

SOLDIER

FRIEND

After the people of God escaped from Egypt, they spent about forty years moving about the desert on the Sinai Peninsula. It took about two hundred more years for them to claim and settle in Canaan, the Promised Land, which they named Israel. The people of Israel set up a kingdom. Their first king was Saul. Their second king was David. During David's reign the Kingdom of Israel flourished.

These passages tell you what David was like—inside and out. When your teacher tells you to begin, read your assigned passage. Circle the word or words that best describe David as he is presented in that passage. Be ready to tell the rest of the group your part of the story of David and to give reasons for your description of him.

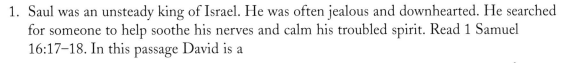

EXAMPLE. The prophet Samuel was sent to Jesse of the house of Judah in Bethlehem to seek one of Jesse's sons to be the next king of Israel (1 Samuel 16:1, 10–13). In this passage David is a

Shepherd   Soldier   musician   Friend   Sinner   king

1. Saul was an unsteady king of Israel. He was often jealous and downhearted. He searched for someone to help soothe his nerves and calm his troubled spirit. Read 1 Samuel 16:17–18. In this passage David is a

Shepherd   Soldier   musician   Friend   Sinner   king

2. David went to the place where the Israelites were at war against the Philistines. He convinced Saul to let him bring down the mighty Philistine commander Goliath with a single, well-aimed stone. Read 1 Samuel 17:48–50. In this passage David is a

Shepherd   Soldier   musician   Friend   Sinner   king

3. In his life David experienced betrayal as well as loyalty, victory as well as defeat. One person who was loyal and attracted to him was a soldier named Jonathan. Read 1 Samuel 18:1–4. In this passage David is a

Shepherd   Soldier   musician   Friend   Sinner   king

4. After the death of Saul, God raised up another person to replace him. Read 2 Samuel 5:1–4. In this passage David is a

Shepherd   Soldier   musician   Friend   Sinner   king

5. When David was king, he arranged to place a commander named Uriah in the line of fire. David wanted Uriah to be killed because he wanted to marry Uriah's wife, Bathsheba. The prophet Nathan confronted David and accused him of adultery and murder. Read David's response in Psalm 51:1–6, 9–12. In this passage David is a

Shepherd   Soldier   musician   Friend   Sinner   king

Consider *Me*

Discover what you and David have in common. When your teacher reads each prompt, write down how you are like David.

1. Like David I can do a lot of things fairly well. I am good at three things:

   a. _____

   b. _____

   c. _____

2. Like David I have had to admit my mistakes and change my ways. This is one time I did that:

   _____

   _____

3. Like David I listen to people I trust to help me. This is someone I trust to give me good advice:

   _____

4. Like David I sometimes take charge. This is one time I was a leader:

   _____

   _____

5. Like David I wonder what God wants me to do. Right now I could use God's help with this situation:

   _____

   _____

Key Understandings

David's Response to God
- David was God's anointed king of Israel.
- David sinned and asked for God's forgiveness.
- David honored God's Covenant with the people of Israel.
- Human beings are responsible for caring for the world.
- David understood that he was God's servant-king.

Bible Facts

- The words to songs are called lyrics. The word *lyrics* comes from *lyre*, which identifies a harplike instrument that was known to David and other musicians of his time. Other instruments used to make music when David was alive were the timbrel (like a tambourine), and flutes and pipes made from hollowed-out reeds. The shofar (a ram's horn) and a metal bugle were instruments used to signal rather than make music.

- Wolves and lions and jackals menaced the flocks of the countryside in Israel. The black lion was a common and very dangerous animal. That lion is now extinct.

- The slingshot David used so well was made of leather thongs with a pouch for a smooth stone. The shepherd swung the thongs overhead to build up momentum. When the stone was released, it usually moved with enough force to kill or wound a small animal or startle a large one.

- In the Gospel of Matthew, the wise men were told that the Messiah would be born in Bethlehem. The Messiah was identified as a ruler who would also be a shepherd. (See Matthew 2:6.)

- In the Gospels people call Jesus the Son of David. The church also sees Jesus as more than David. He is *the* good shepherd who lays down his life for his sheep. He is *the* king whose kingdom lasts forever. He is *the* servant leader.

From the Heart

The Old Testament contains seven wisdom books—Job, Psalms, Proverbs, Ecclesiastes, Song of Songs, Wisdom, and Sirach (or Ecclesiasticus). This collection of wisdom books can help us have an understanding heart.

The Book of Psalms consists of 150 prayers that were said and sung by the people of Israel. These prayers have been around for so long that no one is quite sure where they began. We can imagine that David sang many of them throughout his lifetime. Perhaps he learned some of these psalms by heart as a child.

The Psalms express the inner thoughts and emotions. Through them the people of Israel proclaimed their feelings of sadness and happiness, of loss and victory. These prayers that sang out to God long ago continue to do so because people always need to pour out their heart to God.

Scripture Match

Look up the passage you are assigned. Write the number of the passage in the space that identifies the emotion described in the passage. The following citations are all from the Book of Psalms.

1. 6:7–10 (or Psalm 6:7–11 in the New American Bible)
2. 13
3. 22:1–12
4. 23
5. 33
6. 34:5–6
7. 51:3–6
8. 54
9. 69
10. 70
11. 75
12. 81:1–6
13. 88:14–19
14. 91
15. 102:8–11
16. 130
17. 138
18. 142
19. 150

happiness and joy

trust

complaint and grief

thanks

loneliness

fear and need

forgiveness

Key Understandings

Deep Prayers and Great Ideas

- The Old Testament contains seven wisdom books.
- The wisdom books record the deep feelings and thoughts of the people of God.
- The Book of Psalms is a collection of 150 prayer-songs gathered over the centuries.
- The Books of Proverbs and Sirach consist largely of wise sayings.

SPEAKING FOR GOD

David knew that the Lord was the true leader of the Kingdom of Israel. He knew that his own vocation as king was to help the people be faithful to their Covenant with the Lord. The kings after David lost track of this vocation.

When David's son Solomon became king of Israel, he built a magnificent Temple. However, as the kings followed one after another, they betrayed and ignored the Covenant. The kings allowed the people of Israel to worship the gods of neighboring nations, such as Syria and Egypt. People turned against one another. No one cared about the kingdom as a whole. Everyone cared about themselves but nobody else.

Finally, the Kingdom of Israel split into two kingdoms. The large northern kingdom was called Israel. The small southern kingdom was called Judah.

God called prophets to rise up and speak the hard truth to kings and other leaders. The prophets also spoke words of comfort to those who were ground down by the betrayal of their leaders.

The words of the prophets are recorded in eighteen books in the Old Testament. Most of those books are named after prophets from the time of Israel. Five of those prophets are studied in this exercise.

BETRAYAL

The first prophets could clearly see that kings and citizens alike were betraying the Covenant. God was not being honored; the people were treating one another poorly. The prophets spoke out with anger and sadness in their voice.

Amos

Who. Amos was a shepherd and the owner of a fig orchard.

When. About 750 B.C.E.

What. Amos said that if you are unjust, you will create your own downfall.

Read Amos 2:6–7; 4:1–2; 5:11–12. What did Amos rage against?

_____

_____

Micah

Who. Micah came from southwest Judah.

When. About 725 B.C.E.

What. Micah said that to love the Covenant, you must care for the Lord's people in love and justice.

Read Micah 6:6–8. What did Micah say we must do?

_____

_____

Jeremiah

Who. Jeremiah didn't want to be a prophet. He told the Lord he was too young for such a big job. Once the people got so mad at Jeremiah that they tossed him in a muddy well. A foreigner from Egypt rescued him.

When. 626 to 570 B.C.E.

What. Jeremiah said that worship and justice go hand in hand.

Read Jeremiah 7:1–7. What words of the people of Israel were of no use?

_____

What reform did Jeremiah call for?

_____

Comfort

In 721 B.C.E. the northern kingdom Israel was defeated by invading armies from Assyria. When the southern kingdom Judah fell in 587, many people were taken into exile in Babylon. There the people wept for their homeland. The prophets helped as much as they could. They also spoke for God as they offered words of comfort.

Isaiah

Who. At least three authors wrote the long Book of Isaiah. One of the writers lived in exile in Babylon. This writer's words are in chapters 40 to 55 of the book.

When. About 560 B.C.E.

What. The writers of Isaiah said that God's Covenant will be everlasting.

Read Isaiah 44:23; 55:3–5. How should creation express joyful gratitude for God's saving power?

_____

_____

What did God promise?

_____

_____

Ezekiel

Who. Ezekiel was a priest who lived by a canal in Babylon. Ezekiel mentioned his wife's death in chapter 24, verse 18, of his book; this was the only time Ezekiel mentioned his personal life.

When. About 597 B.C.E.

What. Ezekiel told about the promise of a new relationship between the Lord and the people of Israel.

Read Ezekiel 36:24,26–28. What did God promise that was new?

_____

Key Understandings

Prophets of Truth and Comfort

• After the reign of David, faithfulness to the Covenant became less and less important in the life of the Kingdom of Israel.

• From about 760 to 515 B.C.E., prophets spoke for God and called the people back to faithfulness.

• The prophets often warned, threatened, or scolded the people. They also comforted the people and offered hope for a new future.

• The prophets insisted that the people's Covenant with God demanded works of justice.

Shoulds and Woulds

Read each of these situations, imagine yourself in it, and decide what you will do. Then go to the reasons grid on page 31 and check each box that tells why you made that decision.

Situation 1

I think everyone in our school cheats. The minute Mr. Ebert leaves the room, everybody cheats. He says he trusts us; boy, is he dumb. People have to cheat just to keep up. I know what I will do: . . . I will do this because . . .

Situation 2

If Max says playing the piano is for sissies, I'm going to belt him. I'm short, but I'm wiry and I'm angry. Besides, Max is a loudmouth. I know what I will do: . . . I will do this because . . .

Situation 3

Sally jimmied the lock on the vending machine and emptied out all the candy bars. She's giving them away, and I'm dying of starvation. I know what I will do: . . . I will do this because . . .

Situation 4

Dad says he expects me to come with him to the church basement to sort out and pack clothing for the missions. It's a boring job. None of my friends have to go. I know what I will do: . . . I will do this because . . .

Situation 5

I really think the youth minister at church is neat. He's finally having a party for us at the church next week. My best friends aren't going. They say they've had enough church stuff. I know what I will do: . . . I will do this because . . .

Situation 6

Nan is really nice, but she wears dumb clothes—I mean, really dumb. But I think she is funny, and she makes me laugh. My friends said they don't want me to invite her to my party. They said if she's invited they won't come. I know what I will do: . . . I will do this because . . .

	1	2	3	4	5	6
R e a s o n s						
I want to think for myself.	●	●	●	●	●	●
I want to be a friend of God.	●	●	●	●	●	●
I want to do the right thing.	●	●	●	●	●	●
I want to make and keep friends.	●	●	●	●	●	●

Bible Facts

- When John, the son of Zechariah, grew up, he baptized people and got them ready to welcome Jesus. John the Baptizer announced: "Prepare the way of the Lord. Make straight the path. Fill in the valley and straighten the crooked roads. Everyone will see the salvation of the Lord!" (adapted from Luke 3:4–6 and Isaiah 40:3–5).
- The Gospels refer to Jesus as the Messiah the Old Testament prophets spoke of. For example, Matthew 1:23 says Jesus' name will be Emmanuel, which means "God with us," and Isaiah 7:14 says the same thing.
- Matthew 12:18–20 quotes Isaiah 42:1–2 in describing Jesus as a servant who is so gentle he will not snuff out a smoldering wick or crush a bruised reed.
- In Luke 4:16–21, Jesus comes to his hometown synagogue and says that Isaiah's prophecy (42:1–4) has come true. Jesus announces good news and freedom. He will give sight to the blind and liberty to the oppressed.

Prepare the Way
of the Lord

When all was ready, the Lord God of Israel prepared for the coming of Jesus, the Messiah and Promised One and Son of God. The priest Zechariah learned that his son, John, would be the last prophet. John would announce the coming of Jesus. When John was born, Zechariah spoke this blessing:

68 Blessed be the Lord, the God of Israel.

   The Lord has looked with favor on us.

   The Lord brings redeeming power!

69 The Lord has raised up a Savior in the house of David.

70 This is the Lord's promise given to the prophets of old:

71 We will be saved from our enemies and from all who hate us.

72 The Lord has shown the mercy once promised to our ancestors.

   The Lord remembers the holy Covenant;

73 the Lord recalls the oath sworn to Abraham. . . .

. . . .

76 You, my child, are called the prophet of the Most High God.

   You will go before the Lord and prepare a pathway.

. . . .

78 The tender mercy of God, a dawn from on high, will break upon us.

79 Light will spread over all who abide in darkness and the shadow of death.

   The light of the Lord will guide our feet as we walk in the way of peace.

(Adapted from Luke 1:68–79)